Why Aye Boy!

Mel Phillips

Published by Melanie Phillips - 2006
In association with Access Publishing

ISBN 1905170211

Copyright © Melanie Phillips 2006

The right of Melanie Phillips to be identified
as the author of this work has been
asserted by her in accordance with the Copyright,
Designs and Patents Act 1988

All rights reserved. No part of this book may be reproduced, stored in a retrieval system or transmitted in any form or by any means, electronic, electrostatic, magnetic tape, mechanical, photocopying, recording or otherwise without prior written permission from the author, Melanie Phillips, c/o Access Publishing, PO Box 50, Pembroke Dock, Pembs SA72 6WY

Printed and bound in the UK
By JEM Digital, Sittingbourne, Kent

Cover design and illustrations by
Joelle Brindley

This book is dedicated to
Mam and Neil
and of course
all the people of Pembroke,
especially the locals!

Many thanks to the following people –
Mam, the amazing memory woman!
Margaret
Pam
Prudence
Mr John Russell
and
Joelle, for her wonderful illustrations

The Beginning

I wrote these daft yarns for a bit of fun, and to preserve old tales which might otherwise be lost or forgotten.

If you find yourself saying, "By damn, I had forgotten about him," or "I wonder if they still make them any more?" it will all have been worth the effort!

The Long Dogs
Monkton 1

Pembroke can be roughly divided into three sections. There is the west end which is 'Monkton', the east section which is simply known as the 'East End', and sprawled in the middle, there is 'Orange Gardens' and the 'Main Street'.

My father was born in Monkton and lived there until he was five years old, when the family moved to the East End where they remained for many years. Curiously however, most of his family are buried in Monkton cemetery.

Although my mother and father were both born and bred in Pembroke, their families did not know each other, and that is because there were two distinct and separate junior schools,

'East End Junior' and 'Monkton Mixed'. The East End school started out as a boys' school.

My father went to East End School and my mother to Monkton Mixed. Intense rivalry existed between the two schools and gave rise to a popular rhyme, which went something like this:

"East End Bulldogs sat upon a wall
Monkton terriers came and ate them all." [*]
Of course, the rhyme was then reversed for the opposing school.

If my mum wanted to taunt and aggravate my dad, she would say, "We were afraid to come up the East End because it was full of ol' mad people sitting outside their houses on chairs, looking you up and down and passing rude remarks".

To which my father would rejoin, "We were terrified to go up to ol' Monkton because it was always full of long dogs barking and snapping, and trying to bite lumps out of you!"

A 'long dog' is a Pembroke name for a greyhound, hence the old Pembroke expression, "Hell that kid can run, he was off like a long dog".

A lot of men in Pembroke were out of work,

---

[*] The East End have their own rhyme, in which the 'East End water rats came and ate them all'.

through no fault of their own. Hard times resulting from the depression had left many unemployed.

Men from all over Pembroke, not just Monkton, used to breed long dogs and they raced them at a dog track euphemistically called 'The White City'.

Most long dog owners originated from Monkton, but they had no choice but to use the East End dog track. The White City was near where the Pembroke rugby field is today. All sorts of strange and devious practices occurred there. It was rumoured that some dogs were actually painted, whilst others had lead inserted into their muzzles to slow them down!

By this time my mother worked at Mendus the chemist and her uncle, Bertie Brown, was often heard to plead, "Nancy, you are bound to have something in that chemist shop to make a dog go faster!".

Every Saturday afternoon, men took their long dogs to the top of town for the weekly event. Wary East Enders used to give the dogs a wide birth because the owners deliberately kept them hungry, so that they would race faster to try and catch the clockwork bald hare!

There is a tale told by my friend Pam, who was a resident of the East End, of a cat who was minding its own business curled up on a window-sill belonging to one of the house owners. The story goes that on catching sight of the hapless cat who was snoozing in the sun, a dog pounced forward, and as one local put it, "The poor ol' cat only had three legs and a swinger (a severed leg) and the long dog turned un insid out and et un all a whool".

The White City united Monkton and the East End for a once weekly afternoon, then the two communities parted company and went their separate ways for another week.

Stories of Monkton

Since my mother's side of the family originated from the 'Long Mains' and 'The Millbacks' in Monkton, I thought that I should begin my tales there.

My great-grandfather was called Dick Brown and his wife was called Eliza. My mother was the eldest grandchild and therefore remembers them well.

Dick kept wild birds. It was totally illegal to snare and trap them, but a lot of out-of-work men during the depression in the 20s used to eke out a meagre living by raising and selling them. A cock bullfinch fetched 9d and a hen 6d.

Granfer would save up his 'bird money' (he never touched the house-keeping money) and when he had enough he would take himself off to the Salutation pub known locally as the 'Sally', where he would entertain the clientele by singing for more money. He would get roaring drunk and then wend his way home to a furious Gran, who would rant and rave that he had "shamed her and let her down".

There followed a period of at least three weeks when she refused to speak to or acknowledge him. All conversation was conducted through the medium of Mam's Uncle Bertie, who lived at home.

At the table the conversation went something like this, "Ask your father if he wants another sausage".

"Do you want another sausage?"

"Yes."

"He said yes."

"Ask your father if he wants gravy."

"Do you want gravy?"

"No thanks."

"He said no."

Finally she would relent, but only when he softened her up with a small gift.

Tale 2
Larry Lynx

My grandfather, father of my mother, hated gardening, but out of necessity and duty he religiously dug and turned over his large garden at the Millbacks, which is located at the far end of Monkton.

Dick (Mam's grandad) loved gardening and his large plot was full of redcurrants, blackcurrants all kinds of fruit trees and of course a whole range of vegetables.

On a Saturday afternoon during the Summer months, Pop (as we grandchildren called him) loved nothing better than to watch a cricket match. He was a great Pembroke supporter.

This particular Saturday it was very hot and he did not feel like digging the garden. There was a cricket match on in Hundleton. He had a plot at the bottom of the garden which needed digging and turning over, but he couldn't be bothered.

These were the days before flush lavatories and indoor toilets, and Pop and Gran's toilet was located at the bottom of the garden, away from the house. The contents of the bucket were carefully buried in a designated place in the garden, where it was left to rot and later used as valuable compost. They had rhubarb like umbrellas in those days!

On this occasion, in his rush to get to the cricket match, instead of carefully burying the human waste in the designated part of the garden, he hastily buried the contents in the unturned over patch at the bottom of the garden. Having done this he hurried off to watch the cricket in peace.

He had not been gone long before his father arrived at his door. "Hilda (Gran), where's Willie?"

"Gone to the cricket match, Dick."

"Cricket match, bloody waste of time, he should be here digging and turning over that bottom piece. Well, while I'm here I might as well make a start on it myself."

He started to dig. In these days there was no such comfort and luxury as soft toilet paper, for a start it had not been invented. Instead, your average household had to make do with newspaper cut into squares and placed on a nail behind the lavatory door.

There was a sports writer who wrote for the national newspapers at this time called Larry Lynx. He was famous and well-respected. Pop loved sport and loved to read Larry Lynx whenever he could afford a paper.

Suddenly, Dick shouted from the bottom of the garden, "Hilda, come here!"

She dutifully went out to find him incandescent with rage. "Willie's been burying the bucket here, Hilda. He's been chucking it into this undug plot, the dirty bugger."

"No he hasn't," she said, somewhat defensively. "That's pig shit."

The tines of his garden fork told another story. He waved a piece of shitty toilet paper at her and said viciously, "Pigs don't wipe their arses on Larry Lynx!".

She didn't dare laugh in front of him because as she said, "he was a stern old bugger", but once inside the house she covered her face with her pinny and laughed until she cried.

Tale 3
Monkton Tales

Mam used to love to go over to Long Mains to see her gran and grandad, partly because they had a wireless! Gran was very proud of this acquisition, because hardly anyone in Monkton possessed one. Dick had bought her the wireless as a softener, and to say sorry for bringing shame upon her by coming home drunk from the Sally.

The wireless was a huge affair powered by two massive accumulators, it could be re-charged at Griffiths' garage. On one occasion my grandad said to Mam, "Nancy, go down to Griffiths' the garage and re-charge these accumulators."

"If I go, can I listen to radio Luxembourg and the Ovalteenies when I get back?"

"You know that the wireless is only for your gran and me to listen to the news, and the Sunday service, not that old rammass!"

"Please, Granf"

"Alright, but then you got to go home, 'cos I will be wanting to go to bed."

After exactly ten minutes the wireless was turned off and Granfer started to take his socks off.

"Go on home now, maid," Gran said. "Your grandad has got to get up early." (He worked on the Meyrick estate, where he worked all day in the unhealthy conditions of the lime kilns.)

Gran had a double bed downstairs, whilst Grandad had what was called a 'cupboard bed', which was a bed by night, but then magically folded up to become a wooden cupboard, complete with handles (to save space) by day.

My mother had never seen Grandad get into bed, and it was only when he lay dying and the bed remained pulled down in the middle of the room that Mam realised that Granfer had a bed! She always thought that he had told her to go home of an evening, not because he had to go to work early the next day, but because he was ashamed of the fact that he had no bed, and that he had to stand up all night in the cupboard. She had never seen it pulled down before!

My great-granny and Mam's granny

Opening Medicine

Everybody who lived in Pembroke during the 1930s and 40s firmly believed that if you did not open your bowels at least once a day you would end up in a lunatic asylum. To prevent this dreadful occurrence, you were protected by a huge array of the dreaded 'opening medicines'.

Opening medicines did just what their name suggests, they opened your bowels. There was quite a bewildering selection of them too. My mother can recite them all: bile beans, regulets, castorets, monastery herbs, senna pods and Carter's little liver pills, to name just a few.

My mother tried to avoid visiting her grandmother on a Saturday night, because Saturday evening was dosing evening. "Nancy, have you opened your bowels today?" she would ask.

"Yes, Gran."

"Are you sure? I've just been told today that Joe Seburn's got a stoppage and 'e've been took into hospital. You better have some senna, just in case."

The senna pods used to be steeping on the hob every Saturday night without fail, one might say as regular as regulets. Senna looked a bit like old runner bean pods and tasted like something dead!

"Do I have to have the senna, Gran?" said Mam, "My friend Ruby has syrup of figs and she says it tastes lovely!"

"Her mother's well-off, anyway the end result is just the same. Open your mouth."

So they were scoured out to everyone every Saturday evening, just in case we got a stoppage like Joe Sebern.

Everyone, that is, except Granfer, who made his own laxative tablets from strange secret ingredients known only to himself. No senna for him, he made his own 'jollop', as he called it.

He used to mix the concoction together until it made a stiff dough and then roll the mixture into a long sausage shape. He then pulled off small pieces of the dough-like substance and rolled each one into a tiny round pill shape. These he carefully stored in an airtight jar. His own recipe for avoiding the stoppage.

Tale 4

I cannot take the credit for this next story because it belongs to Phil. His widow has very kindly given her permission to re-produce two stories, and this is the first of them.

Phil lived in an area still known to locals as the Millbacks, a lovely part of Monkton. The lovely spot is right on the edge of a tidal creek known as Quoits Mill.

It was a glorious summer's day and Phil was in plenty of time for work, when suddenly he found that he needed to relieve himself. As it was a very warm day, he decided to leave the toilet door ajar. 'Well,' he thought to himself, 'there might even be time to read a bit of the paper'.

He took the paper to the outside lav with the intention of reading it in peace and isolation whilst he had a relaxing sit-downer.

As he sat, paper in both hands, he felt at one with the world. He then heard the garden gate squeak open, and idly thought to himself, 'That's Mrs L. with the mail'.

After a little while he heard urgent footsteps pounding towards the lavatory door.

Presently, he looked up, and to his shock and horror saw the rear end of Mrs L. backing up on him, all the while grunting and tugging impatiently at her drawers as she almost fell through the door. Phil found himself rooted to the spot and unable to speak, as he felt the two mixed emotions of surprise and fear.

With a sigh of impending relief Mrs L. plonked her ample arse down on what she thought was the seat, only to find that she was, in reality, sitting on Phil's lap.

Their simultaneous screams rang around the privy as Mrs L. hastily hoisted up her drawers and made an ungainly exit, with pee coursing down both legs.

Phil was left in shock and horror, his peace and tranquillity shattered by the arrival of Mrs L.

They never spoke to one another again, both of them too embarrassed to greet the other. Indeed, they crossed over the road when they saw each other coming!

Dreadful memories welled up and burned hot into their very souls, at the thought of the brief encounter.

The Main Street

1950s Pembroke

As everyone knows, Pembroke has only got one main street.

In the summer, when the town is crowded with visitors, you will often be approached by holidaymakers who will say, "Can you direct me to the main shopping centre please?"

To which the stock answer will be, "You're in it."

The visitor then grunts with disgust and disbelief and wanders off muttering, "Do you know, they haven't even got a Woolies!".

Well, we locals are very fond of our main street full of building societies, cafés and stinky knick-knack shops! However, years ago in our grandparents' days, we had a proper main street complete with an upmarket ladies' clothes shop, a men's outfitters, a posh shoe shop, and an excellent general stores.

The general stores was called Simons, and had seats for customers to rest whilst they ordered their groceries.

My brother came home on holiday to Pembroke a few weeks ago, and while he was eating his chilli con carne he turned to my mother and said, "Why didn't we have grub like this when we were kids, Mam?"

To which she replied, "Walter Simon had never seen or heard of a green pepper, that's why. This is Pembroke boy, Wisebuys haven't long 'ad um."

Main Street 2

At Simons, the general stores where you could sit and wait in comfort whilst your groceries were packed in brown bags for you, you could buy loose ham and loose corned beef, and broken biscuits by the pound.

Mr Simon employed a Saturday boy, who was despatched (with the aid of an ancient bike, complete with a basket on the front) to deliver the groceries.

The Saturday boy and I used to 'go with each other', and so when he arrived at Poyers Avenue each week I would be waiting for him.

He would perch me precariously in the basket at the front of the bike and then we would whizz down the Awkward Hill and from there around the Castle Walk. Those were the days!

Haggar's Cinema and Ballroom

Everyone loved Haggar's because it catered for young and old people alike. The upper floor was a ballroom, complete with a well-sprung dance-floor, and the lower floor was a cinema.

Saturday night was dance night and most of Pembroke's younger generation used to flock to the ballroom to see such bands as the 'Merseybeats' and single acts such as 'P.J. Proby', 'P.P. Arnold' and even 'Screaming Lord Sutch'.

The cinema was very popular and well attended. There was even a Saturday Matinee which was full of screaming kids who revelled in the weekly serials and cowboy films. There never seemed to be any parents about, but nobody killed each other or damaged anything, except for some kid from the green, who, for some reason known only to himself, used to spit on the screen every week!

The cinema seemed to have been built backwards, so you actually entered through the exit, with the screen behind you. I never really understood why that was.

If you went to the pictures on a Saturday night, you had to compete with the pounding feet which emanated from the dance-floor above!

However, we were much luckier than the people of Pembroke Dock whose cinema (The Grand) had a tin roof. Every time it rained all the action on the screen was drowned out by the pelting rain hammering on the roof!

Pembroke Main Street 3

Next to Haggar's came Hall the baker, then Williams the shoe shop, always known as 'Rosie Bachelor's', because she was the manageress.

Next door was Williams the plumber, followed by Bagshaws, who sold almost everything.

The next shop comprised a strange combination of two very different commodities. This premises belonged to a Mr Pike. His was a double-fronted premises. One side of his shop was devoted to selling everyday chinaware, whilst the other side of the shop sold toilets and lavatory seats.

My grandad was very clever at composing rude rhymes and he made up one for Mr Pike and his emporium.

"Mr Pike, Mr Pike you can say what you like
But your window is truly a farce.
In one side you have cups and saucers,
And in the other a place for your arse!"

After Mr Pike came George Mason. Before it was George Mason it had been the Star Supplies Store, but when I was a child it was George Mason.

I have an abiding memory of George Mason. My brother and I were each given 1 shilling and 6d pocket money a week, which my father doled out to us every Friday night. My brother always had to spend his cash all in one go. At this particular time, he had developed a passion for glace cherries. He blew the whole of the 1 and 6d on a massive bag of the sticky things. Once home he raced up to the confines of his bedroom and consumed the whole bag at once. He then became violently sick, had a hiding from Dad for wasting his money, and to my knowledge has never eaten a glace cherry since.

Mr Brown's The Chip Shop

Mr and Mrs Brown had a tiny fish and chip shop, before they moved to the bigger premises across the road, where it still remains today. The best fish and chips then, and still the best now!

Melias

'Melias' owned a chain of shops and stocked a good variety of provisions.

Mr O. was the manager of Melias and he had an assistant called Derek, who was about the same age as my mum.

This particular day my granny had detailed my mother off to Melias for a pound of fat sausages. Her thin sausages she got from 'Eastman', the butcher's across the road.

"A pound of fat sausages, Mr O," my mother said.

"Sorry 'un," he guffawed, "we've a run out. The only sausages here are mine and Derek's."

Derek flushed bright red and my mum, who was very naïve and innocent, went back home and said, "Mr O. said that he has run out of sausages and the only other ones he's got belong to him and Derek."

With that, Gran flew into a rage. "The dirty old swine," she said. "That's the last time I go into Melias!"

The Miss Townleys

Two sisters, always referred to as the Miss Townleys, owned a very good wool shop. These were the days when every wife was expected to know how to knit, and had been taught the skill by their mothers. My mother attempted to teach me to knit but I was hopeless, lacking as I was in domestic skills.

I was fascinated by the sisters' wool shop. The wool was everywhere. It was stacked high on the shelves in tidy plastic bags and piled up on the floor. The Miss Townleys sat calmly and serenely in the midst of their wool, often knitting themselves, all the while in conversation with a customer.

One of the sisters, I don't know which one because to me they looked exactly the same (although they were not twins), gave piano lessons. The 'better off' parents used to send their children for lessons with Miss Townley, whether they wanted to learn or not.

My friend Pru and her brother Clive were forced kicking and screaming up to town after school for their lessons.

Pru would shout after me as I played on the swings opposite her house, "You lucky sod, you can stay here and play in the park!"

Main Street 6
The right-hand side of the town

Opposite Simons, on the right-hand side of the road, was Mr Davies' the chemist. My grandad used to be a Saturday boy for Mr Davies.

Mrs Davies was a very fussy and particular woman. She used to call my grandad 'Brown'.

On a Saturday morning she very often sent him over to Mr Morris the butcher for lean pork chops. My grandad would duly come back with the meat and she would inspect them thoroughly and pronounce them "too fat". Granfer was then supposed to take them back to look for leaner ones.

He used to cycle around the commons and then back to the chemist's shop with the same chops, where Mrs Davies would run her beady eyes over them and say, "That's better!"

Percy Rees

Not far from the Castle Inn, where Tenovus is now, there was an excellent ladies' clothes shop.

They only sold the best quality clothes and the service was second to none. When Percy's had a sale, people would queue outside waiting for the doors to open.

In the 70s, when I was teaching in Oswestry, my mum queued outside Percy's to buy me a harlequin jumper which I had been admiring.

I proudly wore that jumper when I went to teach at Pembroke School a year later.

Almost at once one of the horrors in my class stood up and said, "Hey Miss, you look like Bertie Bassett!"

It didn't put me off it though, and I wore it for many years, until it fell abroad.

Hancock's Offices and Off Licence.

After this came a very special dwelling house, complete with two separate offices, which were owned by Hancock's Brewery but occupied the same premises. This is where my family lived. The Georgian building now belongs to Robert the hairdresser.

In the 18th Century it belonged to Robert George and Co. Brewers. Mr George's bottling plant was called the Cromwell Brewery and was situated where the Haven Church is now.

Twenty-nine Main Street became Hancock's Offices and Off Licence, with the off licence on the left-hand side of the building and the offices on the right.

The flat upstairs was given over to the manager of Hancock's. When a manager retired or died, the flat passed to the new manager.

My dad had been an employee of Hancock's since he was fourteen years of age and so in 1967, upon the death of Mr Rees, the old boss, my dad became the new manager of Hancock's. Our family moved from Poyers Avenue to the flat above the two premises.

The flat was huge and had exactly 39 steps from top to bottom, just like John Buchans' book!

Mam decided that the whole place needed re-decorating, and as it was the summer holidays, my brother and his friend Colin were detailed off to strip what was later known as the 'big room' of its many layers of paper.

The idea was that Neil would first dampen the walls with a pump-action device, and then use the scraper to loosen the layers of old paper.

They soon got bored with this. The pump was fun to use, especially if you soaked your mate with it, but the difficult scraping was hard work and no fun at all.

Eventually they stopped working, and after a while opened the sash windows wide on to the street below.

From this vantage point they directed the jet of water on to men's bald heads as they passed underneath. They squealed with delight and glee at the plight of the poor unfortunates, who became soaked with a blast of freezing cold water. The two of them would then duck quickly down beneath the window-sill and wait for the next victim, their theory being that people rarely look upwards.

However, one bald-headed man was too fast for them. Soaking and fuming with rage he stormed into the office downstairs, and demanded to see the manager, to whom Neil and Colin's antics were revealed.

They waited in trepidation for the inevitable rant, which would definitely ensue. My father was furious. "I didn't pay you two lazy buggers half a crown an hour to mess about up here!" he yelled. "Now bloody well get on with it and let's have no more arsing about!"

They sheepishly returned to their work and the room was finally stripped of its layers of ancient wallpaper.

Our family spent many happy years at 29 Main Street, and we had many a raucous Christmas party in the big room.

Mendus the Chemist

Next to 29 Main Street was, and still is, Mendus the chemist.

It was not until recently, when another chemist had taken over the premises and kept the name Mendus, that I realised the significance of the name, which had to be pointed out to me. For those who are as slow to catch on as me, the name 'mend us', makes a perfect name for a chemist shop!

When my mother left school she went to work for Mr Mendus. Mr Mendus was a very clever man and had two degrees to his name. One was in ophthalmics and the other was a pharmaceutical degree. Consequently the front of the shop was a chemist whilst the rear of the premises was an optician's.

My mother used to help Mr Mendus with the opthalmics and also helped the second chemist, Mr Rees, with the dispensing of drugs and medicine. She also served in the shop when required.

She was serving in the shop one day, when a gentleman came in and asked to see Mr Rees the chemist. My mum replied that Mr Rees was at lunch and asked if she could be of any assistance. He said that it was alright and that he would wait for the chemist to return.

He sat and waited, his eyes alternating between the clock on the wall and the front door as if he was willing Mr Rees to walk through it.

Finally he could wait no longer, and hastened towards the counter.

Averting his gaze, he turned to mother and said, "A packet of condoms please."

My mother duly served him and he hurried away with his purchase.

He came in every week after that and Mam would discreetly wrap his condoms up in a brown paper bag.

One particular day she saw him approach the counter and anticipating his purchase, she wrapped the condoms and handed them over to him.

He shuffled his feet in an embarrassed manner and said shyly, "I only want milk of magnesia tablets this week."

Chemist 2
Old Farmer

Many farmers who could not afford a visit from the vet would come into the chemist to buy various powders, potions and drenches, with which to treat their animals.

One morning, an old Pembroke farmer came into the Chemist's shop and asked for a ball for his sheep dog.

My mother, who was serving behind the counter at the time, said, "We don't stock those, you'll have to go to Bagshaw's shop across the road."

To which he replied, somewhat tartly, "A WORM BALL, GIRL!".

Orange Gardens

Orange Gardens is what you might call a suburb of Pembroke. It is very cleverly laid out in a network of streets, which are based on the grid system. Orange Gardens used to be a little community all on its own. It had its own shop-come-taxi business, and its own members-only club called the Black Rabbit. The club still remains today and continues to prosper.

I was brought up in Orange Gardens, and lived in Paynter Street until I was twelve years of age.

Our family lived in one of the 'prefabs'. Prefabs, or prefabricated dwellings, no longer exist, as they were temporary housing erected after the war when housing was scarce. They were only supposed to have a lifespan of ten years, but people lived in them for far longer than that.

The council built one hundred prefabs in all, eighty-four in Britannia Street, Pembroke Dock and sixteen in Paynter Street and Jogram Avenue in Pembroke.

They were very well appointed and there was a waiting list to have one. They had built-in bathrooms, fridges, and even fold-away ironing boards. People were jealous!

The only trouble was that, like caravans, they were freezing in the winter (so much so, that icicles formed inside the windows) and boiling hot in the summer, due to the asbestos attracting the heat.

The Prefabs and Rough Ground

It was great growing up in the prefabs. Most of the occupants were recently married couples, and most of them had children the same age as me and my brother.

There was a piece of disused ground opposite our house, and this became the play area for all us kids.

We named the derelict piece of land 'rough ground', and on rough ground we always built our annual bonfire for Guy Fawkes night.

The bonfires always took on the same shape, that of a wigwam. They were well constructed by the older boys and were completely dry and cosy inside. Old tyres purloined from Campbells' garage were carefully piled up the outside of the bonfire.

However, the fire had to be guarded at all times lest the East Enders or even the Monktonites infiltrated rough ground and whipped our tyres. The guarding of the fire was a serious business and the responsibility of the older boys. They would even work shifts throughout the night every night until November the fifth, to make sure the thieves from either side of town didn't pinch their precious booty.

Of course, at the same time, Monkton and the East End were also keeping all night vigils in their bonfires, in case the rough ground gang struck and made off with *their* stash of salvage!

Rough Games 1
Prefabs 2

We played some very rough games. The pavement which surrounded the prefabs was a circular one, so it was possible to peddle your bike, skate, or skip all the way around it.

My Uncle Ken worked for Davis Steel, a factory in Pembroke Dock, which made, amongst other things, roller skates, which were the must-haves of our day.

All roller skates made at the Davis Steel factory had rubber wheels, but sometimes mistakes were made by employees, and the reject skates were given to the local kids. My Uncle Ken gave me and my brother two pairs of roller skates with steel wheels and no rubber grips! These were magic, you could hurtle around the block with sparks flying off the steel wheels, and easily outstrip those kids who had rubber ones. Unfortunately, they were very dangerous, as well as being extremely noisy.

On the right-hand side of our prefabs were some private houses, mostly occupied by older residents who had lived peaceably in Paynter

Street long before we came along and destroyed their harmonious way of life.

One of these residents was a Mr D. Poor old fella, he must have had a culture shock when our families moved in!

Mr D. had his own solution to noise pollution. He would wait for us to come flying around the corner by his house and as we drew alongside his door, he would throw out a coconut mat and stop us in our tracks. We would trip headlong over the mat and skin our knees on the pavement and on the rough fibres of the coconut. We would then limp home bawling and howling to Mam, who would exclaim, "Serve you both right, I've told you about annoying Mr D." before adding, "Miserable old bugger!".

Rough Games 2

Next to our street was Jogram Avenue. The two streets used to run into one another, but today they are separate.

At the end of Jogram was what we all called 'the bank'. The bank is still there today and is a steep, dangerous field, which descends straight on to the main road beneath.

It was on the bank that I first learned to ride a bike, the hard way.

A friend of mine who lived in the posher houses across the way from me had an old sit-up and-beg bike. "Come on," she said one day, "come on up the bank and I'll teach you how to ride my bike".

I duly went with her, and she held the seat for me as I tentatively began to peddle.

"Don't let go of the saddle, will you?" I said.

With that I heard a maniacal laugh, and I turned around to find myself alone and flying towards the main road. She had let me go!

Before I reached the bottom, I flung myself off the bike, scraping my knees and suffering grass burns to all visible parts of my body.

"What the hell happened to you?" Mam asked when I got home.

"Janet let me go down the bank," I wailed.

"What did you go and trust her for, you know she's a bit light (soft in the head)."

And that was all the sympathy I got.

Rough Games 3

Orange Gardens had the best park, East End had an apology for a park and Monkton didn't have one at all.

The park is still there on the commons but it is a shadow of its former self.

The park had something which ordinary parks did not have. It had a relief pond, which was built to stop the commons from flooding. The pond was like an ornamental lake and even had an island in the middle, which was home to nesting swans.

The channel of water, which still runs the full length of the commons, we called 'the lake', and the lakes were referred to as 'the pond'.

When the schools broke up for holidays we would all spend our days in the park, only returning home when we were hungry. Parents never came looking for us.

Kids regularly fell into the pond, went home soaking wet, had a hiding, got changed, and came back out to play.

We turned over and over on the swings, and fell off on to the concrete, we crashed and bashed the witches' hat roundabout into its pole in the middle so hard that it made our teeth rattle and our bones reverberate. We covered the slide with candle wax and whizzed down at a rate of knots, only to go shooting off the end and on to the hard-baked grass.

The see-saw stood on a concrete base, and it was great fun to pile about six kids on one end and shove one poor weak little 'un on the other end, so he would go shooting up in the air, landing on the concrete below.

Rough Games 4

We climbed huge pine trees and covered our clothes with resin, which never came off and always stained.

We swung across the lake on a rope, clearing it.

We played a really dangerous game called 'splits', which involved two knives, and played 'touch on it' with a cricket ball!

All mothers were into violence, and not only bashed their own kids but other peoples' too.

"Mrs Pattison hit me, Mam."

"You must have deserved it."

You never questioned her reasoning, you just got on with it.

And to think that these days they play conkers with gloves on, to stop the hard nut bruising their knuckles.

Huh!

Pop and Gran

My gran and grandad lived in Orange Gardens, at no. 3 South Road, right next to Argents building yard.

They had moved from the Millbacks in Monkton because, due to an increased family, they needed more room.

Her name was Hilda and his was William, but to the family they were known as Tilly and Willy.

They never socialised, and never went out visiting, they led totally insular lives.

Their conversation involved news of the family, what they were having for dinner, and my grandfather's caged birds.

Pop

Adults called my grandfather Witty Brown. Us kids just called him Pop.

He was called Witty because he was so funny. He worked for the R.E.M.E as a blacksmith, mending army trucks etc. He also did ornamental blacksmithing, such as wrought iron work.

He was a small, wiry man. He wore plaid lumberjack-type shirts with the sleeves rolled up, revealing a tan which stopped just above his elbows.

Behind his left ear there was always a half smoked 'Craven A' fag. He would always take just two drags, then nip it for later.

He whistled continuously.

Unlike my gran, he was indifferent to food. His idea of heaven was a plate of homemade chips with runner beans, and a piece of white bread and butter.

He had a very weak stomach and would leave the room if someone ate a runny egg or poured parsley sauce over their boiled ham!

He was essentially a very shy man and if strangers or neighbours visited the house he would take himself off to the woods to look for useful stout sticks or to gather seeds for his wild birds. He mainly collected hardheads which is a Pembroke name for those stiff-stemmed plants with brown seedy heads (the lesser knapweed).

Pop's Class

Anybody recognise their grandfather?
I can't say for sure which one is Pop.

Pop's Birds
Pop 2

Pop kept goldfinches, greenfinches, bullfinches and canaries in a shed at the top of the garden. He would send away to Norfolk for the canaries, and they would arrive by train.

He crossed the canaries with the greenfinches, hoping to one day produce the perfect mule, with the green body of the finch and the yellow wing-tips of a canary, but he only ever succeeded in raising little dull brown birds.

When it was feeding time he would have to change his clothes into ones which the birds were familiar with. Consequently, he always wore a long leather waistcoat, the same old patched trousers, and his flat hat turned back to front.

Sometimes he would allow me and Neil into the inner sanctum of the shed, but you had to promise to be very quiet. On these occasions, if you were lucky, he would strike his anvil and the birds would recognise the sound and start singing.

Pop would enter his birds in the local wild bird competitions, for which all birdcages were required to be painted regulation green.

My grandfather was colour blind, and on one occasion he took great care over the painting of his display cages, only to be told by my grandmother that he had painted them all red!

After one particular show he came home in a furious temper. He had a prize bullfinch, which he felt sure would win. Alas, he was beaten by some rogue from the East End who had cheated and painted his 'bully's' chest a glorious red. The paint washed off in the rain, but it was too late. The villain had won the cup!

Pop 3

My grandfather used to make up rhymes to make my brother and I laugh. He could only do this when my grandmother was well out of the way!

Here are some typical ones.

"Not last night but the night before
Two tomcats came knocking on my door.
One with a fiddle and one with a drum
And one with a pancake stuck to his bum!"

"I am going to Upper Lawton,
Where the hares roost
And the hens fly backwards,
To keep the dust out of their eyes."

We would scream and squeal with laughter, until Gran would shout from upstairs, "Willy, are you telling those kids rude rhymes?".

He had wonderful sayings too. If two ugly people got married, he used to say that they were "a mate for the owl".

If he spotted someone who had a really bad back and couldn't stand up straight he would say, "I saw Georgie Phillips in town, and uh was bent over like an S hook."

And my favourite, "I see that old Mary G. from West Street is engaged to that nice'll boy Hopkins from Orange Gardens. I wouldn't have her if her arse was stuck with diamonds."

Pop The Hoarder
Pop 4

Pop and Gran were hoarders, but he was worse than her. "You never know when you'll need one," was his philosophy.

When they died and the contents of the house was sorted out, my uncles and aunts found heaps of old army blankets under the mattress of their bed. It must have been like a chapter out of that story 'The Princess and The Pea'.

Pop would love to go to auctions where there were house clearances. He bought most of the furniture for no. 3 South Road from auctions. My uncles tell the tale of when he went to Bowlings Auction Room. It was raining heavily outside and there was a leak in the roof. A stranger happened to be next to my grandfather. The man tried to dodge the drips by putting up a large umbrella, as he did so, the auctioneer, thinking that he was bidding, knocked down a cardboard box full of dirty, stinking cake tins to him!

If Pop could get a bargain, or something for nothing, he was made up. He was 'very careful with his money', as Pembroke people say. A euphemism for mean or tight.

He acquired a set of hair clippers and charged trusting friends 6d a time to give them terrible haircuts.

He never accepted decimalisation and described it as a "fad which would soon die out". Or he would say, "I can't do this ol' money, why don't they wait for the old 'uns to die first and then bring it in. That would make more sense."

His love of hoarding lives on in my auntie. When we were cleaning out his house, she waved a will form aloft, and said, "Anyone want a will form? It's brand new, shame to throw it away".

Faux Pas
Pop 5

I must inherit my effortless ability for making faux pas from Pop. Pop was truly a past master.

There was a time when he was talking to his next door neighbour over the hedge, when a pitiful specimen of a cat wandered into the neighbour's house. "Good God, Mrs Barratt!" he exclaimed. "A stinking, manky, bald cat with a tail like a bottle brush has just gone through your passage."

"Why, Mr Brown, that's our Fluff!" she replied.

Then there was the time when he was in the doctors' waiting room. The doctor was late beginning his evening surgery, so he struck up a conversation with the woman sitting next to him.

"Where are you from?" he asked.

"Golden Hill," she said.

"Ah, that used to be a nice l'l place to live, before that stinking, dirty S– family moved up there."

"I am Mrs S," she replied angrily.

My grandfather looked at her in horror before racing out of the surgery. He never did get to see the doctor.

Gran

Gran was rotund and obsessed with food. In fact she was the complete antithesis of my grandfather.

She was either making food or eating it. As you walked in through the door, the first thing she would say was, "What's your mother got for dinner?".

She made wonderful rough puff pastry, like Chelsea buns and Eccles cakes. She also made Chester cake, which is not often made or sold these days. She also made fantastically fat pancakes. So fat were they, that when you bit into them, teeth marks were left behind. In fact everything she made was fat, except for bread. Bread was never bought, sliced bread. It was white and baked by Brawn.

I used to watch her cutting bread. She would somehow place the loaf under her chin as if she was about to play the violin, and cut around the loaf with a very thin, worn and lethal sharp knife. She cut perfect thin slices, which she piled high on to an awaiting plate.

The butter dish was next to the bread. It contained a block of local butter called Arbeston Road. It was wrapped in thin grease-proof paper, was bright yellow, and sweated droplets of salt and fat. It tasted wonderful. Never mind the cholesterol, that hadn't been invented!

Gran's Animals (Dogs) 1

They weren't really Gran's animals. Pop brought them home, but she ended up looking after them.

The first dog was born over in the Millbacks and was called Nell.

Although she slept in the house, she was essentially a working dog.

Pop also used to keep ferrets, which he used to flush the rabbits from the warren. Nell would then pick the rabbit up in her soft mouth and return it to Pop.

When my mum was a kid, she would spend hours dressing the ferrets in doll's clothes, only for them to wriggle free in a trice.

Pop could play the mouth organ. Nell would be sleeping quietly in front of the fire whilst Pop played tunes on the organ. He could play any tune he liked except 'The Little Grey Home in the West'. As soon as he started to play she would sit bolt upright, throw her head back and howl!

Nell died and a procession of dogs followed. Pop had no more working dogs. Then along came Chips.

Chips was a cairn terrier. He was not a very prepossessing dog. He wasn't very trustworthy either and had a tendency to bite, especially kids! All in all he didn't have a lot going for him.

He was grey in colour and suffered rather badly with dermatitis. He was continually scratching and spent most of his time underneath cars, where he used to rub his back raw trying to rid himself of his constant itching. His skin condition was mainly due to his extremely poor diet.

Gran's Animals 2
Chips

Gran got it into her head that Chips didn't like dog food. He did, it was just that Gran was too mean to buy him any. He had the odd tin of 'Lassie' if he was lucky, and sometimes some dried meat from Radnor's shop, but other than that, he lived on eggs! Gran would say, "Chips is hungry, I think I'll fry 'un an egg." Or "I think I'll make Chips some pancakes."

She would then make one of her extra fat pancakes and Chips would down it in one! No wonder his hair fell out.

If we went to the beach, Chips had to come too. Pop and Gran couldn't drive, so my dad was usually landed with him.

Once at the beach he would dive into the water and chase the seagulls. When he tired of that, he would drink copious amounts of sea water.

On the return journey the dog would be wedged in the back with the family. The cry would inevitably go up, "Chips is hawking!" Dad would then have to stop the car for Chips to be sick.

He would get out of the car and rage, "That's the last time that bloody dog is coming in my car!".

Chips 3

My uncle liked to go foraging in the woods looking for birds' nests, mushrooms and blackberries.

This particular day, he was going for a walk on his own, when Gran shouted after him, "Take Chips for a walk".

"No."

"Go on, he loves a walk."

Finally, he relented, and they began their walk up Grove Hill.

When they reached the top of the hill Dick looked round to find that Chips had got fed-up and walked home.

Dick continued to walk until all of a sudden it started to pour with rain. He hot-footed it back home as fast as he could, but still managed to get soaked through to the skin.

When he got indoors, he found Chips curled up on the mat. My uncle swore that he looked at him and smirked. He knew that it was going to rain!

Ben the Cat

Pop loved cats. He would bring home wild ones from the wood. They were nearly always vicious and had to be kept outside, because they were not house trained. Some chased after rabbits, only to have their legs torn off and mangled in gin traps.

This particular day Pop brought home a lovely wild ginger kitten.

My Uncle Steve was only about two years of age at the time and wouldn't leave the cat alone. Gran decided that the poor little thing needed some peace and locked him in the lavatory. When she went to check on him later he had drowned in the toilet!

Ben was not wild. He came from my Auntie Susie's farm in Llandyssul. Susie came on a visit and brought with her a tabby cat for my Auntie Molly (whom she named Rocky) and a black and white kitten which was given to Gran and Pop. Pop called him Ben.

Ben was affectionate and clever. My grandfather would roll the silver paper from his 'Craven A' packet into a ball and then throw it for the kitten who would retrieve it and bring it back to Pop.

Poor Ben. He fared little better than Chips in the food stakes. He was never given cat food. Instead, he survived on a diet of bread, water and Marmite all mixed together like sop.

He did not last long. He was run over trying to cross the Watery Lane. He was probably too weak from hunger to get out of the way of the car!

Gran's animals
Roger

Roger was a green budgie. He was a present for my Uncle Steve on his tenth birthday. He was called Roger because the day that he took up residence at 3 South Road, Dr Roger Bannister had run the mile in under four minutes.

His home was in the 'middle room', in his cage perched atop a long stand.

Above the budgie's cage was a large framed print called 'Napoleon Surrenders to Great Britain'. I loved this picture. It was taken from a famous Victorian picture by Sir Philip Orchardson. I loved his grumpy face as he looked out to sea, on his way to St Helena. Whenever I went to Gran's house, I would ask, "Gran, can I go in and see Roger?".

Gran would reply, "Yes, but if I catch you swinging his cage around again, you'll have a hiding".

I would stand underneath the cage on its long stand and stare up at Napoleon, who was on his way to prison and entrapment. I idly wondered if Roger felt the same way. It didn't stop me giving his cage a twirl as I went out though.

When my gran and grandad died and the possessions were all divided up amongst the family, someone asked me what I should like. I answered, "Napoleon".

He hangs in my hall to this very day.

The East End

It has been written that in Victorian times the East End of Pembroke was "full of thieves, rogues, and vagabonds".

Well, my father's relatives met none of these criteria. They were very religious, and were stalwarts of Mount Pleasant Baptist, which sadly, is no longer a chapel.

Grandfather did not smoke, drink or read a newspaper on a Sunday, although he would read the same paper on a Monday!

My brother and I went to Sunday school. We had to go because all my relations (except for Dad) attended.

I remember the austere building, lacking in any ornamentation, the 'Sankey' hymns, and the Pastor, a Mr Morris. All the ladies wore old fashioned fox fur hats, with the paws dangling about their throats, and big costume jewellery brooches. They trilled and warbled when they sang.

My brother could never keep still during the long sermons and was continuously being told off by my Auntie Peg. "Be quiet, Neil."

"Can we go now, Auntie Peg?"

"Not yet."

"Show us your teeth then."

We were fascinated by her teeth. She had two false ones on a plate. The only way she could keep us quiet was to drop down her two front fangs. We would shudder, and, temporarily satisfied, keep quiet for a little while longer.

The Harvest Festival

Every year at the beginning of October we had the Harvest Festival.

Everyone was expected to donate something. This particular spring, Dad gave Neil and I some marrow seeds.

"Here you are," he said, "we will have a competition for the Harvest Festival. We will see who can grow the biggest marrow in time for the harvest".

This was wonderful fun. We watered and nurtured the marrow seedlings, and they thrived. The only snag was that mine grew much bigger than Neil's.

One day, he came rushing into the house and blurted out, "Dad, Dad come quick, the slugs have had Mel's marrow!".

Dad went out into the garden to inspect the damage. The marrow had certainly been damaged, but it was not the work of a slug. There was a very neat hole bored into it, but the top skin of the vegetable was at the bottom of the hole.

"Funny slug that," said Dad. "It goes and leaves the skin from the top down at the bottom of the hole. What did you poke it with Neil? And don't tell me any lies".

"A bamboo stick, Dad."

He had a good hiding, but that was no consolation to me. My marrow withered and died, and his continued to flourish, and went on to win top prize at the harvest!

The Passion Play

Every year the Baptist chapel re-enacted the Passion and Miracles of Christ. Auntie Peg always wrote the script.

I was ten and my brother Neil was nine when we were dragooned into acting in the play. I was to play the part of Jesus, Neil was John the Baptist, Mary Richards of Golden Hill was selected to play the part of Mary Magdelene (because she had long hair), and Glyn Thomas from Orange Gardens was the leper. There were other members of the cast, but I cannot bring them to mind.

My brother was in his element as John the Baptist, because Auntie Peg had made him a kind of cave man loincloth to wear, which had been fashioned out of an old fur rug. He insisted on cutting his own staff, which he and Pop had hewn from Bowett wood. Around his head he wore an old towel secured with cord.

I had to wear a long white draped sheet which reached to the floor, sandals, the mandatory head gear, and a headband, which was far too big for my head.

The leper wore his ordinary clothes, because he had been away on holiday and Auntie Peg had had no time to make him a costume.

My poor mother was detailed off to watch the performance, whilst my dad was 'far too busy' scoring cricket matches for Pembroke!

"It's your relatives, Mervyn," my mum would bawl. "I'm Church (Monkton), you ought to be there, not me."

He would then sigh, and explain patiently to my mother as if she was a child, that you could not begin a cricket match without a scorer and that his presence was required. Indeed it was imperative that he attend. He could not let the boys down.

The Passion Play Continued

The eager congregation settled itself down, and the play began.

There was trouble from the beginning. My headgear kept falling across my eyes, making it impossible for me to see, without continuously pushing the band up.

Mary Magdelene washed my feet. Her long hair tickled me, and I burst out laughing. The headband kept on slipping. By this time Auntie Peg was giving me threatening looks and the ladies of the chapel were not amused. The only person bursting with suppressed mirth was Mam.

My brother made a grand entrance, holding his staff in his outstretched hand. The trouble was that he used his free hand to scratch himself, because his 'raiment' was itchy. Throughout his speech he continued to scrawl and dig at himself. However, worse was to come.

"All hail!" he bellowed, and proudly held his staff aloft. Unfortunately the staff was too long, and as he raised it, he smashed the chapel light on the left-hand side of the altar to smithereens.

My Auntie Peg groaned, and prayed that nothing else would go wrong. She reckoned without the Leper. He had his arm up the sleeve of his jacket, feigning a diseased limb.

I touched him and said in a confident voice, "Go forth, your faith has made you whole."

With that, the Leper shot out his arm, and accidentally punched me straight on the nose.

The play was a disaster. My Aunt was upset, and the congregation embarrassed. All, that is, except for Mother.

When Dad came home from the cricket match she said, "Merv, you missed a treat, it was better than a 'Brian Rix' farce!"

Neil and I were never asked to take part again.

The Sunday School Treat
Baptist 2

I always envied my friend Prudence.

She attended St Mary's Church, and they always broke up from Sunday school for the school summer holidays. Just as I laughed about her having to go to music lessons, so she had the last laugh when I had to dress up to go to the Baptist during the summer.

They also had a marvellous church treat. They went to Broadhaven, or Angle. We went to Pendine!

If you attended our Sunday school regularly, you were entitled to attend the treat, but some would worm their way in by attending for about four or five weeks before.

We were driven to Pendine (I have a pathological hatred of the place to this day) in Silcox's 'matchbox' bus.

My grandfather had a springer spaniel called Peter. He used to bring Peter on the treat, much to the dismay of every passenger.

Peter had had distemper when he was a pup and although he had recovered, it had left him with St Vitus' Dance. This meant that he could not control his muscles. He twitched continuously. This, however, was not the main cause of the problem. He stank, it was like the dog equivalent of B.O.

We used to pick Granfer and Auntie Peg up at Station Road and you could hear people on the bus muttering before they got on, "I hope Tom Phillips isn't bringing that stinking dog".

Of course he always did. No one liked to voice an opinion about the 'stinker', because Granfer was superintendent of the Baptist.

It nearly always rained on the treat. If by any chance the weather turned warm, by the time you walked to the sea over the ridged sand, which hurt the soles of your feet, it was time to go home.

When the day was done, we all piled into the local Sunday school tea room. The tea was always the same. Slab cake from the Star Provisions in Pembroke, seed cake (ugh), Scribona fruit pies, (the poor man's Lyons tart), hot tomato sandwiches, and sticky sweets in cone shaped bags.

Adults drank tea, and children glugged Tosco pop (poor man's Corona).

Everything was packed up and Mother would say, "Bloody good job that's over for another year."

East End Primary school

East End Primary was my school. Now it is called 21C and Global Connection, and is in danger of being knocked down.

It was a great school and a tough one! I was only four and a half tears old when I started. We were in Miss L.'s class. She turned out to be a vicious old bird who would cane you for looking at her the wrong way.

On the first morning we all took our seats and awaited instructions.

"Hands up who wants milk," she said, in a waspish little voice. We duly put our hands up, all that is, except for one little boy.

"Do you want milk, boy?" she snapped.

"I wants red pop," he said, with great confidence.

She scrutinised him with her beady little eyes before shouting, "What do you think this is boy, a cafe?".

Playtime

We had two separate playgrounds. One for the boys and one for the girls. However, as no teacher ever seemed to be on playground duty, it was very easy for all of us to flit from one playground to the other.

We played all sorts of dangerous games, but the most unhygienic was the 'urinal game'!

This entailed crossing over into the boys' playground and doing all manner of acrobatics and gymnastics, using the urinal cubicles as parallel bars!

We were fit. We skipped and turned somersaults, stood on our heads using the concrete playground as a gym mat and chased each other around the playground.

Education

We return to the former East End School, Pembroke, again this week for this group of children photographed in 1960. All placings are left to right. Back: Mr Crichton Reynolds (a member of the teaching staff who later became headmaster of Cosheston School), R. Arnold, R. Britton, W. Griffiths, A. Hodge, G. Asparassa, R. Broad, G. Scourfield; 3rd row: N. Scourfield, C. Gibby, M. Waters, A. Smith, S. Richards, M. Phillips, P. Patterson, M. Jackson, M. Lewis; 2nd row: R. Parsons, D. Haggar, L. Hay, M. Lewis, J. Hazier, L. Phillips, M. Handley; front: B. Kromrei, J. Jenkins, J. Clarke, G. Jones, R. Evans and N. Campodonic.

The old school was cold in the winter. We had open fires in the classrooms, but the teacher stood and warmed his backside in front of it, so no heat ever came our way.

We had gas lighting. This fascinated me because the teacher lit them every morning with a lighted taper.

In the infants we had slates and chalk to write with. If you were lucky you could be made a monitor for the day. A slate monitor's job was to give a slate and a piece of chalk to everyone. If you hated someone enough, you would get your own back on them by giving them a shiny slate, so that they would have to wet the chalk every time they wrote a word!

Your parents supplied you with a chalk rag, which was kept up your sleeve. When you finished your work, and the teacher had marked it, you simply rubbed it out and started again. Teachers did not keep records in those days. The only document kept religiously was the register.

Other monitors included the milk monitor. Two children were chosen for this task. First of all, you had to arrange all the thirds of a pint of milk around the fire to warm. This done, one of you stabbed the silver milk tops with scissors to make holes in them, whilst the other inserted a straw into the apertures.

In the juniors, the most coveted job was ink monitor. This job also required two people. The ink came in powder form and needed to be mixed up in a metal jug with just the right amount of water. Not too much, because that would make it too runny, and not too little as this made it lumpy. Then, using the jug, you very carefully filled up every inkwell. You used the ink to dip your 'dip pen' into. Whilst one child sorted out the ink, the other was busy cutting up the pink blotting paper into small squares.

Sometimes Miss would ask you to fill her inkwell on the big desk with red ink! This was indeed the greatest privilege of all.

The Staff

After a year in Miss L.'s class, we were taught by the lovely and gentle natured Mrs L. She and the kindly Miss B. used to walk to school across the commons, and hordes of kids used to fight to carry their bags. Miss L. and Miss J. used to walk too, but they were left alone, nobody offered to carry their stuff.

When we reached the age of seven we became 'top infants' and thought we were king pins! There was one draw back if you were a top infant. You had to share your classroom with the lower infants.

It was a wonder that we learned anything at all, because you had two different age groups being taught two different subjects in the same room! There was not even a partition. How did we concentrate?

Miss J. taught the seven-year-olds. She was a stout, brusque, cruel woman, who only seemed to possess two dresses.

There was a two-tier system in her class, which comprised those who were good scholars and those who weren't. She had no time for slow learners, who were literally left to their own devices. All her attention was directed at the better pupils.

We even had two different types of furniture! The top set had lovely shiny new tables, and the poorer set had desks which were falling to pieces.

Mrs J. used strange words like 'galoshes', instead of 'wellies'. One day I turned up late for her lesson. It had been raining and I was carrying a little pink umbrella, I was also wearing wellies. "Hurry up, girl, you're late," she bellowed. "Put all that paraphernalia in the corner!"

I went home that night and asked Mam, "What's paraphernalia?"

"Why do you want to know?" she said.

"Miss J. told me to put my paraphernalia in the corner."

"She classes one umbrella as paraphernalia!" exclaimed Mam.

The Juniors

When you became a top junior, you could lord it over everyone else. Top juniors were divided into two classes. Mr R.'s class or Mr N.'s class.

You were expected to work very hard in these two classes, because these were the eleven plus classes.

After being groomed for the mock exam, you had to sit the real eleven plus in the grammar school on the hill.

I still remember the Silcox bus which took us there, and the sense of fear when we arrived at the seemingly huge and imposing building. Small wonder then that some children failed the test, they were terrified out of their wits.

The results were awaited with baited breath. Some kids had even been promised a bike if they passed.

Primary school eventually ended and it was time to go to the 'big school'. Friendships were broken for ever as we were split into groups, one destined for the grammar school and the other to secondary modern.

Last Story
The Old Man from Thomas Street

The last story in the collection should belong in the Orange Gardens chapter, but I thought that I should end this collection of tales with a raucous ripper of a yarn.

This is Phil's second story and ranks as one of the best.

Many years ago there was an old man who lived on Thomas Street in Orange Gardens. He was a regular at the Black, so much so that he practically lived there.

The old fella had a long-suffering wife called Lil. She frequently threw his ruined dinner in the bin when he had decided that he would prefer to drink at the club than come home at a decent hour and spend time with her.

This particular Sunday night, his downtrodden and miserable wife had had quite enough of his antics, and decided that she would confront him as soon as he set foot inside the door.

She began her rebellion by vehemently throwing his dinner in the bin. She then sat herself down in the chair and waited for him to fall drunkenly through the door. This time she had made up her mind that she would leave him.

Just before 10.30pm (chucking-out time) she heard him noisily open the front door.

"What's for dinner, Lil?" he bawled.

"Arseholes!" she said, angrily.

To which he replied, "Well, just fry one for yourself!"

The Conclusion.

Well, the long dogs have long gone, and so has The White City.

The Main Street has lost its array of fine shops.

The prefabs, rough ground, the Sunday school treats, and East End School are mere memories.

Let's hope that the Pembrokeshire dialect lives on.

Of course it will.

Why Aye Boy!

About the Author

Mel Phillips was born and bred in Pembroke. She taught for thirty-two years altogether, seven years of which were spent in Pembroke Comprehensive and sixteen years in Pembroke Dock Primary, which later became Pembroke Dock Community School, also known as 'The Big Blue School'.

Mel's interests include shooting, computers, swimming and going to Pembroke Leisure Centre gym. She has been in the Cross Saws pub quiz team for 20 years and is a volunteer in the South Pembs Hospital, for the Pembroke Dock Stroke Association and also the Pembroke Dock Gun Tower.

Mel lives in Pembroke, with her mother just round the corner. Her brother Neil, also a retired teacher, lives in Buckinghamshire.

Illustrations by Joelle Brindley
Freelance Illustrator and Animator

If you would like any more information or would like to contact her:
Tel: 07887 513908
Email: joelle@off-kuff.co.uk